The INSIDE & OUT GUIDE *to*

INVENTIONS

CHRIS OXLADE

Heinemann
LIBRARY

CONTENTS

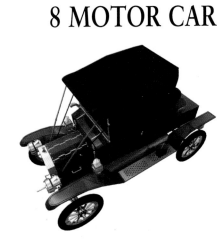

The INSIDE & OUT *GUIDE to*

INVENTIONS

CHRIS OXLADE

THE INSIDE AND OUT GUIDE TO INVENTIONS
was produced by

David West 👫 **Children's Books**
7 Princeton Court
55 Felsham Road
London SW15 1AZ

Designer: Rob Shone
Illustrator: Alex Pang and Moorhen Studios
Editor: Dominique Crowley
Consultant: William Moore
Picture Research: Victoria Cook

First published in Great Britain by Heinemann
Library, Halley Court, Jordan Hill, Oxford
OX2 8EJ, part of Harcourt Education.
Heinemann is a registered trademark
of Harcourt Education Ltd.

11 10 09 08 07
10 9 8 7 6 5 4 3 2 1

10 digit ISBN: 0 431 18305 8 (hardback)
13 digit ISBN: 978 0 431 18305 3
10 digit ISBN: 0 431 18312 0 (paperback)
13 digit ISBN: 978 0 431 18312 1

British Library Cataloguing in Publication Data

Ganeri, Anita, 1961-
Inventions. - (The inside & out guides)
608
A full catalogue record for this book is available
from the British Library.

Printed and bound in China

PHOTO CREDITS :
Abbreviations: t-top, m-middle, b-bottom, r-right,
l-left, c-centre.

Pages 12t & b, 15m – NASA; 16t, 21t, 25t – Library
of Congress; 6t – Thameside Local Studies and
Archives; 9t – Mercedes Benz Classic; 14t – Ray
Hooley, oldengine.org; 15t – Western Front
Association; 17t – reproduced courtesy of Museum
Victoria; 18t – Science Museum, Science & Society
Picture Library; 19b – Hong Kong Graphics and
Printing; 23t – Marcus Kaar, portraitkaar.at; 24t –
John Jenkins, sparkmuseum.com; 24b – David Wort;
26b – Sony United Kingdom Ltd.; 27t – NMPFT,
Science & Society Picture Library; 29t – Dr. Ing Horst
Zuse

Every effort has been made to contact copyright
holders of any material reproduced in this book.
Any omissions will be rectified in subsequent
printings if notice is given to the publishers.

*An explanation of difficult words can be
found in the glossary on pages 30 and 31.*

INTRODUCTION

An invention is a new machine, a new tool, or a new way of doing something. Over thousands of years inventions have changed the way we live. They help us to work, travel, and manufacture things. Inventions entertain us, help us grow food, and enable us to find out about our world. Some inventions come from a flash of inspiration, when an inventor has an idea. But most are the result of many years of hard work.

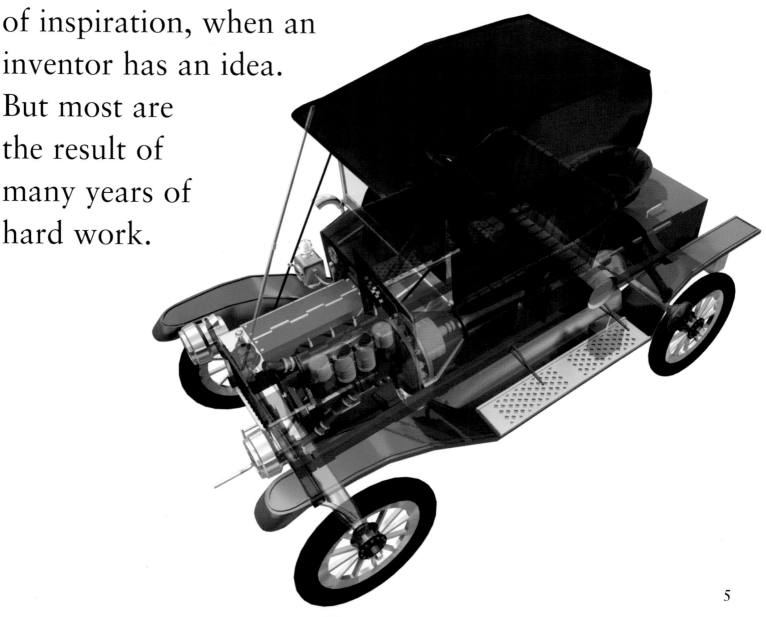

STEAM ENGINE

STEAM PROVIDED THE POWER FOR the very first type of engine. At first, these simply pumped flood water from mines. Inventors put steam engines on wheels, and the steam locomotive was born.

NEWCOMEN'S ENGINE
In 1712, Thomas Newcomen built his first beam engine. The piston moved one end of the beam. The other end operated a water pump.

Early steam engines did not move. They were too big and heavy to drive locomotives. Lighter, more powerful steam engines were developed in the early 1800s, and soon the first steam locomotives appeared. The *Rocket* (right) was built in 1829 by British engineers George Stephenson (1781–1848) and his son Robert (1803–1859). *Rocket* won the Rainhill Trials, a competition held to find a locomotive to pull trains on the new Liverpool and Manchester Railway in northern England. *Rocket* won because it had a multi-tube boiler. This invention allowed *Rocket* to make steam faster than its rivals.

Water barrel

Tender

TREVITHICK'S LOCOMOTIVE
British engineer Richard Trevithick (1771–1833) built high-pressure steam engines for pumping water from mines. In 1804, he put one of his engines on wheels, making the world's first steam locomotive.

FIREBOX

Burning coal or wood in the firebox made hot gas that flowed into the boiler tubes. Fuel was stored in a box called the tender.

Fuel

CYLINDERS

Steam from the boiler was fed to the cylinders. The steam pushed the piston out and then back in again to turn the drive wheel.

Boiler

STEAM **EXHAUST** OUTLET

Exhaust steam from the cylinders was fed into the smoke stack. This flow of steam helped to pull heat from the firebox through the boiler tubes, heating the water.

Smoke stack

Steam valve

Boiler tubes

BOILER

Water in the boiler was heated by hot gas from the fire flowing along the boiler tubes. The heat turned the water to steam.

Drive wheel

MOTOR CAR

appeared on the roads in the 1880s. This was the start of a transport revolution. Twenty years later, a huge motor industry was up and running. Cars were being produced in their thousands.

BENZ MACHINE

This is a Benz car of 1888. It has three wheels because it was based around a horse-drawn carriage. This is why early cars were known as 'horseless carriages'.

The motor car became possible when the **internal combustion engine** was invented. The first engines were not powerful enough to move a car. But in the 1880s, German engineer Gottlieb Daimler (1834–1900) invented a small, lightweight, four-stroke **petrol engine**. Daimler built his first car in 1887. Cars were rare until **mass production** began. Small, cheap cars such as the Ford Model-T (right) then became available.

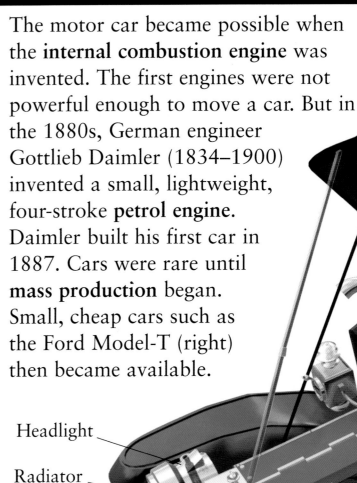

Headlight

Radiator

ENGINE
The Model-T had a four-cylinder petrol engine. It could produce about 20 horsepower.

Starter handle

FORD PRODUCTION LINE

Henry Ford (1863–1947) was a pioneer of mass production. He designed the Model-T to be made cheaply on a production line. Until then, cars had been made one by one.

GEARBOX
The Model-T had three **gears**. There were two forward gears and one reverse gear. The driver selected the gears with foot pedals.

Hood

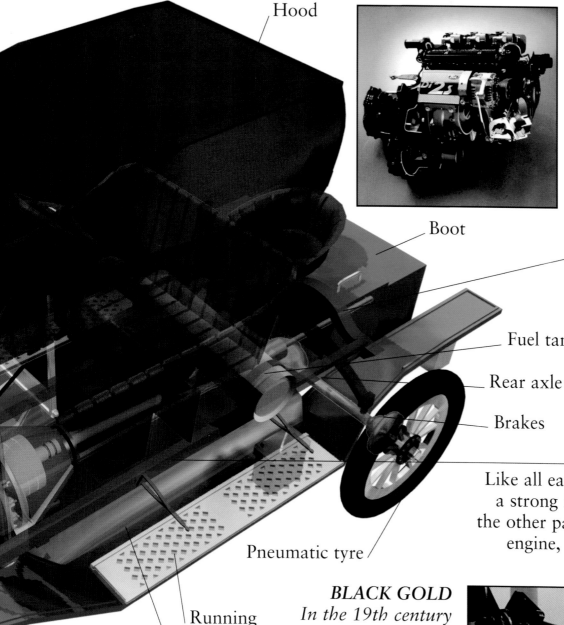

TWO AND FOUR STROKES

In a four-stroke engine, each cylinder fires on every other downstroke. In a two-stroke engine (left), it fires on every downstroke. Four-stroke engines are more efficient.

Boot

SUSPENSION

The Model-T had one suspension spring on the front axle and one on the rear axle. The wooden wheels had **pneumatic** tyres.

Fuel tank

Rear axle

Brakes

CHASSIS

Like all early cars, the Model-T had a strong frame called a chassis. All the other parts of the car, such as the engine, body, and fuel tank, were bolted to the chassis.

Pneumatic tyre

Running board

BLACK GOLD

In the 19th century oil was known as 'black gold' because it made people rich. Without the supplies of petrol made from oil, the motor industry might have failed.

BODYWORK

The body was made from metal panels bolted to the chassis. The fold-down fabric hood was raised in rainy weather.

PLANE

MANY UNLUCKY INVENTORS WERE INJURED OR KILLED TRYING to fly with strap-on wings. It was not until the 19th century that the science of flight was understood. Aviators developed wings and invented ways of steering aircraft through the air.

LILIENTHAL GLIDES

*Otto Lilienthal (1848–96) studied bird flight before building a series of **gliders** in the 1890s. He made more than 2,000 flights before he was killed in a crash.*

One of the first planes to fly was a simple glider built in 1849 by British engineer Sir George Cayley (1773–1857). At the time, there was no engine light enough to lift a plane into the air. The Wright brothers built their own petrol engine for their famous *Flyer*, which made the first-ever controlled, powered flight in 1903. A modern, state-of-the-art plane, such as the F-35B strike fighter (right), uses many of the inventions developed since the first planes flew. These include the autopilot, the jet engine, **radar**, and vertical flight, where a plane can move up and down in the air, without needing to move forwards.

Stabilator

Fuel tank

RUSSIAN GIANT

*Many modern planes such as the giant Antonov An-225 cargo plane are powered by a type of jet engine called a **turbofan**. The jet engine was invented by British Royal Air Force officer Frank Whittle in the 1930s.*

EXHAUST NOZZLE

Exhaust from the engine comes out here, pushing the aircraft forwards. The nozzle is swivelled to point downwards for vertical flight.

F-35B STRIKE FIGHTER
THE **F-35B** IS A
'STEALTHY' AIRCRAFT. ITS
SHAPE MAKES IT ALMOST
INVISIBLE TO ENEMY
RADAR SYSTEMS.

Orville Wright
(1871–1948) and Wilbur
Wright (1867–1912) made
hundreds of test flights
with kites and gliders
before building Flyer.

STABILISING NOZZLES

During vertical flight, a nozzle under each wing blows engine exhaust gas downwards. The flow of gas is carefully controlled to keep the aircraft stable.

Rudder

Folded
undercarriage

Fuel
tank

Weapons
bay

Gun

LIFT FAN

The F-35B is a short take-off and vertical landing (STOVL) aircraft. The **thrust** for vertical flight is produced by a fan that is covered by doors during normal forwards flight.

COCKPIT

A mass of electronic equipment helps the pilot fly, **navigate**, and use the F-35B's weapons. The pilot can see information about the plane's systems on a computer screen inside his helmet.

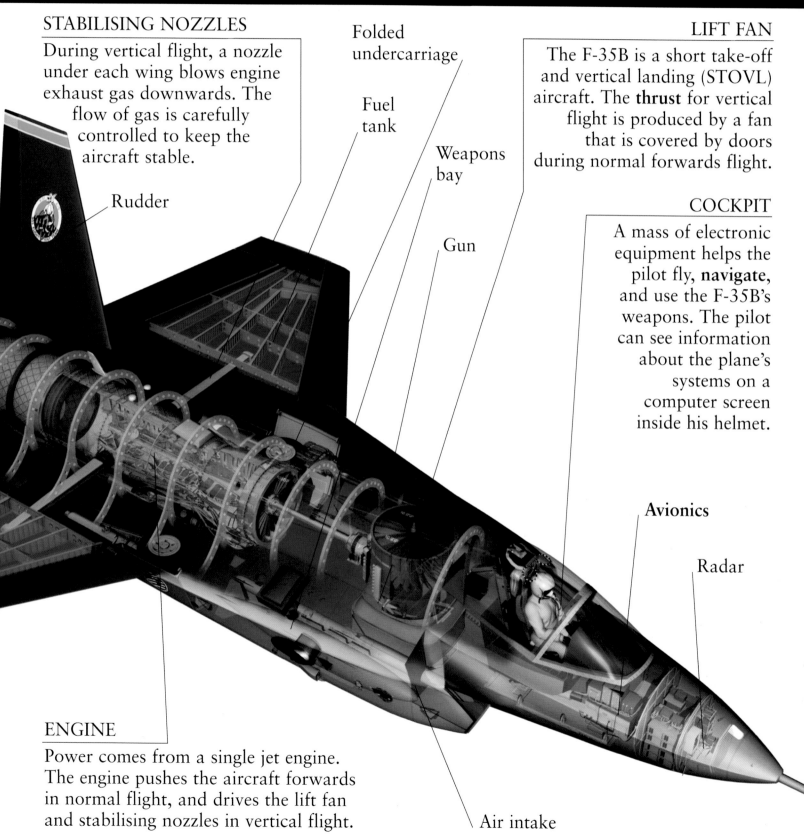

Avionics

Radar

ENGINE

Power comes from a single jet engine. The engine pushes the aircraft forwards in normal flight, and drives the lift fan and stabilising nozzles in vertical flight.

Air intake

ROCKET

FIREWORK ROCKETS
A firework is a solid-fuelled rocket. Inside is a powder that burns, making gas that shoots the rocket into the air. The rocket explodes when the fuel runs out.

A thousand years ago, the Chinese used rockets as weapons and as fireworks. These rockets used gunpowder as fuel. A rocket with solid fuel, such as gunpowder, is called a solid-fuelled rocket. All rockets were solid-fuelled until American rocket pioneer Robert Goddard (1882–1945) invented the liquid-fuelled rocket. This design contains liquid fuel and a supply of **liquid oxygen**. The two liquids burn when they mix together. A liquid-fuelled rocket is easy to control because the flow of fuel can be altered. Goddard launched his first rocket in 1926. His invention led to the development of the V2 rocket, a weapon used in World War Two. Liquid-fuelled rockets reached space in the 1950s.

FUEL

The V2 had two fuel tanks. One contained a mixture of **ethyl alcohol** and water, and the other liquid oxygen. With the maximum amount of fuel on board, the rocket's range was 320 kilometres.

Ethyl alcohol and water tank

WARHEAD

The V2 could carry a tonne of high explosive to its target. The explosive was detonated by a trigger when the nose hit the ground.

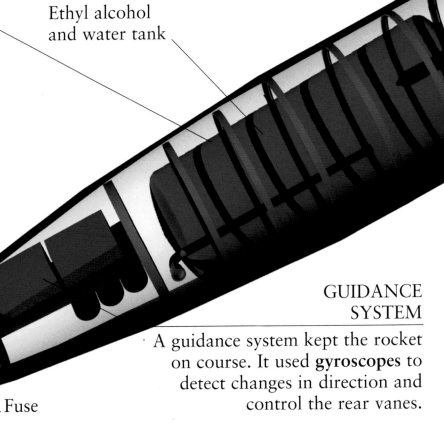

Fuse

GUIDANCE SYSTEM

A guidance system kept the rocket on course. It used **gyroscopes** to detect changes in direction and control the rear vanes.

V2 ROCKET
THE GERMANS USED THE V2 TO BOMB ENEMY CITIES. MORE THAN 3,600 V2S WERE LAUNCHED BETWEEN 1944 AND 1945.

Wernher von Braun (1912–77) developed the V2 rocket in Germany in the 1930s and 1940s. After World War Two he moved to the USA, where he worked on long-range military rockets and space rockets.

STABILISERS

Four stabilising fins kept the rocket flying straight. There were two small control vanes on each fin. These were turned from side to side by the guidance system to make small adjustments to the direction of flight.

ENGINE

Fuel and liquid oxygen were pumped into the **combustion** chamber through 18 nozzles. They mixed in the combustion chamber, where the fuel burned, creating hot gases that rushed out of the exhaust nozzle. This stream of gas pushed the rocket forwards.

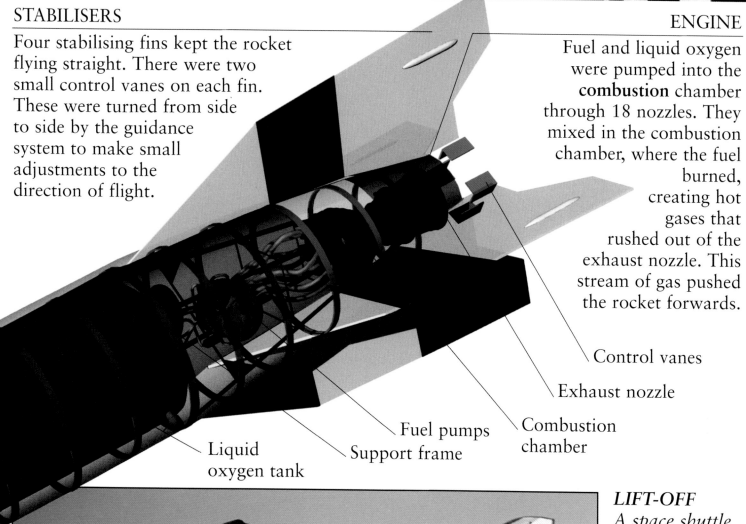

Control vanes

Exhaust nozzle

Combustion chamber

Fuel pumps

Support frame

Liquid oxygen tank

LIFT-OFF
A space shuttle orbiter has three liquid-fuelled rocket motors. The fuel is stored in the giant tank underneath the orbiter. The shuttle needs an extra push for take-off, which comes from two solid-fuel boosters.

TANK

THE TANK MADE ITS FIRST APPEARANCE DURING WORLD WAR One. This new fighting machine, with its squealing tracks, heavy machine guns, and thick heavy armour, must have been a terrifying sight on the muddy battlefields.

The first tracked vehicles were developed in the early 20th century. They were used as farm tractors. At the beginning of World War One, Ernest Swinton (see page 15) had the idea of a tracked fighting machine. It would be able to drive through muddy fields, break through barbed wire defences, and cross trenches. This would clear a path for troops. The first British tank was tested in 1915. A year later, the Mark I tank went into battle. Early tanks often broke down or got stuck in mud, but by World War Two, the tank was an important weapon.

FIRST TRACKED MACHINE
The 1905 Hornsby chain tractor was the first **self-propelled**, *tracked vehicle. The tracks spread its 10-tonne weight over the ground, stopping it from sinking into the mud.*

TRACKS
Each track was made of metal links (called shoes) joined together to make a continuous loop.

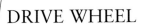

Drive chain   Gears

DRIVE WHEEL
A large rear wheel on each side drove the tracks round. Teeth on the wheel interlocked with holes in the track.

MODERN TANK UNITS
The tank is vital to a modern army. Tank units attack enemy tanks and support infantry. An advanced electronics system makes a tank's gun very accurate.

MARK I TANK
TANKS GOT THEIR NAME
BECAUSE PEOPLE BUILDING
THEM THOUGHT THAT
THEY WERE MAKING
WATER TANKS.

Ernest Swinton (1864–1951) was a British army officer. He realised that a tracked fighting machine could break the stalemate of trench warfare. His idea was put into practice in 1916.

SHUTTLE MOVER
Giant tracked vehicles called crawler-transporters carry space shuttles to their launch pad. Each one has eight enormous tracks.

ARMOUR PLATING
The Mark I had side, roof, and front armour to protect against machinegun fire. This was made up of steel plates 12 millimetres thick.

STEERING
The driver steered left and right by braking on one track or the other.

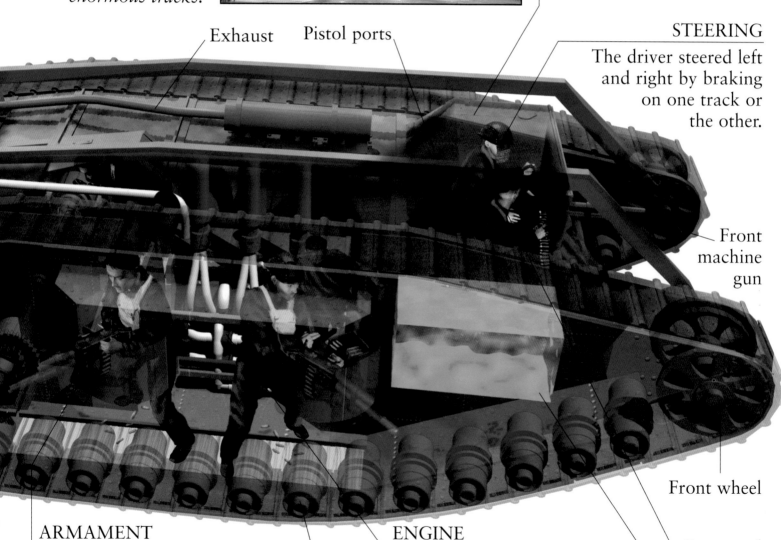

Exhaust

Pistol ports

Front machine gun

Front wheel

Command post

Fuel tank

Idler wheels

ARMAMENT
This Mark I tank was armed with six machine guns. Other models had two artillery guns and four machine guns.

ENGINE
The tank was driven along by a huge Rolls Royce 105-horsepower engine. But because the tank weighed 28 tonnes, its top speed was only 7 km/h.

FARM MACHINERY

THREE HUNDRED YEARS ago farming was done by hand. Today, machines such as tractors, seed drills, and combine harvesters plough fields, sow seeds, and harvest crops with great speed.

Harvesting a crop means reaping (cutting the stalks), threshing (knocking the seeds from the stalks), and winnowing (separating the seed from the straw and chaff). The first threshing machine was invented in 1786, and the first successful reaping machine in 1851. In the 1880s, Hugh Victor McKay (see page 17) combined a reaping machine, threshing machine, and winnowing machine to make the first-ever combine harvester.

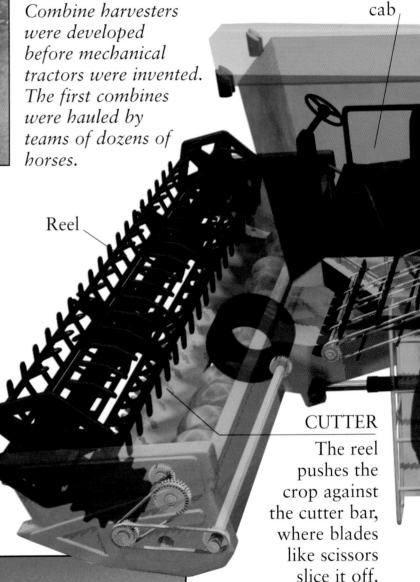

HORSE POWER
Combine harvesters were developed before mechanical tractors were invented. The first combines were hauled by teams of dozens of horses.

Air-conditioned cab

Reel

CUTTER
The reel pushes the crop against the cutter bar, where blades like scissors slice it off.

HARVEST TIME
At harvest time, combine harvesters move into the fields. They remove the grain from crops such as wheat and corn. They store the grain and dispose of the straw and chaff.

Hugh Victor McKay (1865–1926) was operating a winnowing machine on his father's farm in Australia when the idea of a combine harvester came to him. He was just 17 at the time. He called his new machine the Sunshine Harvester.

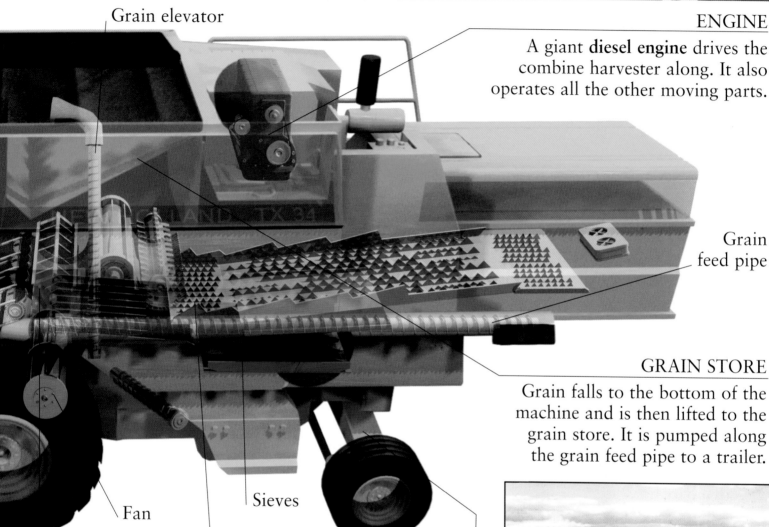

Grain elevator

ENGINE
A giant **diesel engine** drives the combine harvester along. It also operates all the other moving parts.

Grain feed pipe

GRAIN STORE
Grain falls to the bottom of the machine and is then lifted to the grain store. It is pumped along the grain feed pipe to a trailer.

Fan

Sieves

AUTO-LEVELLING AXLE
The rear axle tilts from side to side to keep the combine harvester level. This stops the grain from sliding to one side.

THRESHING CYLINDER
The cut crop is carried up to the threshing cylinder by a moving belt. Here, it is squeezed and beaten to knock off the grain. Most grain falls through sieves.

STRAW WALKERS
The straw moves along vibrating plates, which allow any remaining grain to fall through. Underneath, a fan blows the chaff from the grain.

PEA PLANTER
This tractor is pulling a pea-planting machine, which levels the soil, drills holes, and plants the seeds. It takes its power from the tractor.

PRINTING

Copying a letter or a book was a long and difficult job before printing was invented. A person called a scribe made every copy by hand. The invention of printing and copying machines allowed many copies to be made very easily.

The first printing process was called letterpress printing. Pictures or words were carved into wood. The blocks were inked and pressed on to paper. Later, metal letters called type were put together to make words. The photocopier made copying documents much more convenient. The photocopier was invented in 1938 by American law student Chester Carlson. It used light and **static electricity** to produce a copy.

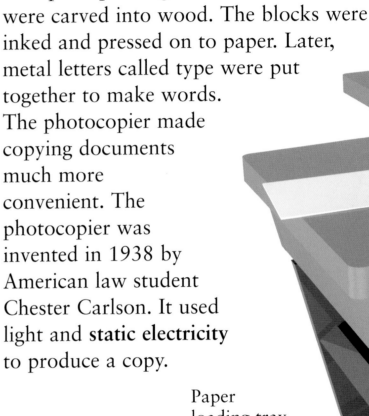

CHINESE PRINT BLOCK
More than 3,000 years ago, the Chinese were printing with carved stone or wood blocks.

Paper loading tray

Feed rollers

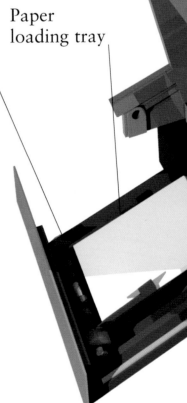

MODERN PRINTING
This book was printed on a machine like the one shown here. The four colours that make up all the others are printed in turn. It can print over 10,000 sheets of paper an hour.

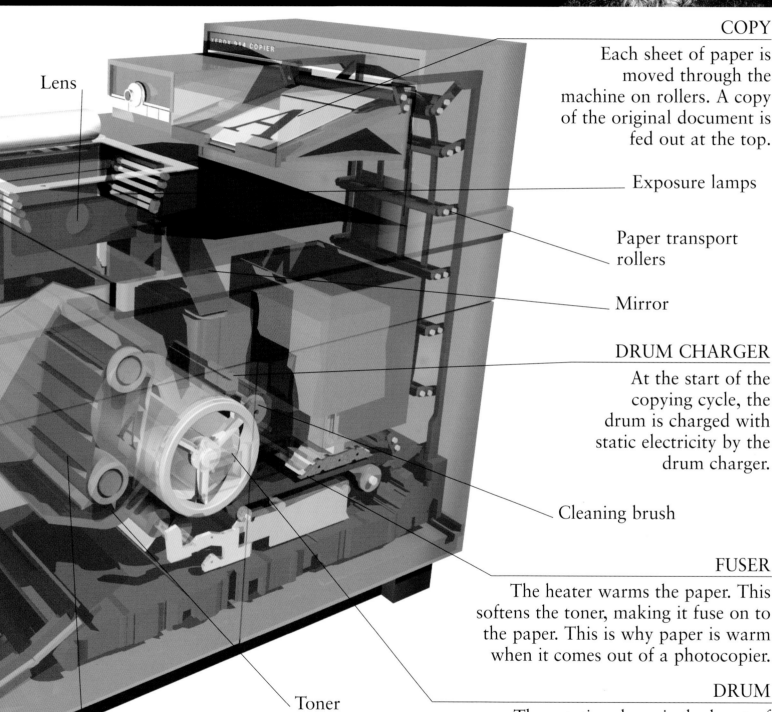

Lens

COPY

Each sheet of paper is moved through the machine on rollers. A copy of the original document is fed out at the top.

Exposure lamps

Paper transport rollers

Mirror

DRUM CHARGER

At the start of the copying cycle, the drum is charged with static electricity by the drum charger.

Cleaning brush

FUSER

The heater warms the paper. This softens the toner, making it fuse on to the paper. This is why paper is warm when it comes out of a photocopier.

DRUM

The rotating drum is the heart of the machine. Light from the document shines on to the drum via mirrors and lenses. The more charge that the drum contains, the darker the printed document.

Toner

TONER FEED BELT

The toner brush puts toner, a coloured powder, on the drum. The toner sticks to areas that are still charged, printing a copy of the original.

TELEPHONE

Two inventors patented the telephone on the same day in 1876. They were Alexander Graham Bell (see page 21) and Elisha Gray (1835–1901). They both worked out how to make a microphone, which allowed sound to be sent along a wire. Bell formed the Bell Telephone Company in 1877.

The first telephone systems had just two telephones, with a wire between them. Two years later the first telephone exchange opened in New Haven, USA. Gradually exchanges were linked together, forming the first telephone **networks**. The first hand-held mobile telephone was developed in 1973 by Motorola. The first **cellular** telephone networks opened the following year. Since then, handsets have become smaller and more complex, and the networks can now carry media messages, such as pictures and digital data, as well as sound.

CENTRAL PROCESSOR
The processor controls the phone by carrying out programmed instructions. The instructions are stored in the phone's memory.

THE FIRST PHONE
This is a copy of Alexander Graham Bell's telephone of 1876. The tube on the left was both the mouthpiece and earpiece. The central section turned sound into electricity and back again.

CAMERA
This is a camera phone. It has a small lens with a light-sensitive microchip behind. Images and video are stored in the phone's memory and can be sent to other phones.

BATTERY
A rechargeable battery powers the antenna that sends radio signals to the network.

SCREEN

The display is a high-resolution, liquid-crystal, thin-film transistor (TFT), colour screen. It is used to show the phone's menus, photographs, video, and information such as battery life.

SWITCHBOARDS

The first telephone exchanges were operated by hand. Modern exchanges are digital, and are part of a huge communications network.

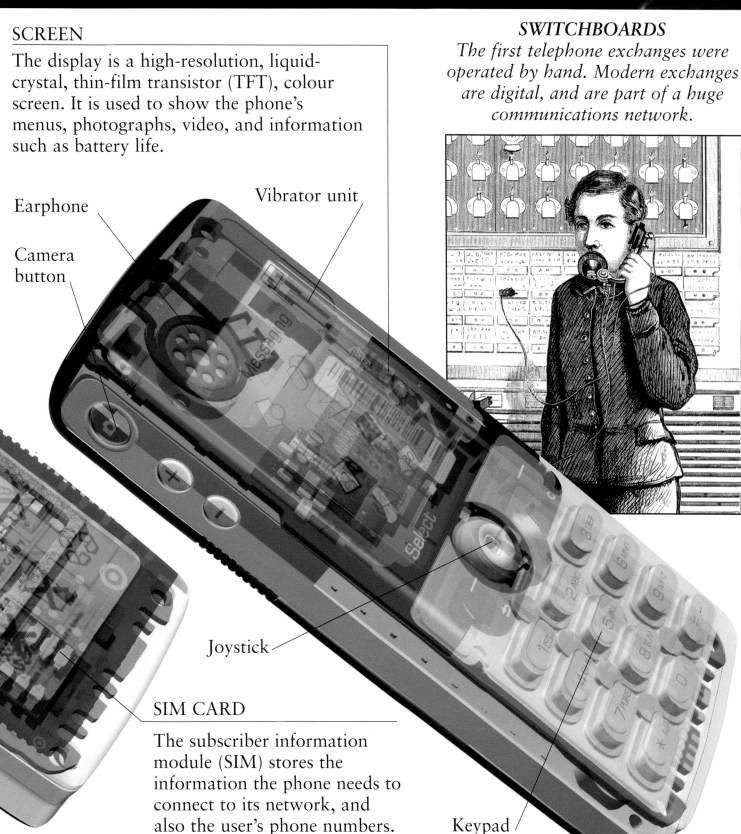

Earphone

Camera button

Vibrator unit

Joystick

SIM CARD

The subscriber information module (SIM) stores the information the phone needs to connect to its network, and also the user's phone numbers.

Keypad

TELESCOPE

A TELESCOPE IS AN INSTRUMENT THAT MAKES distant objects look larger. The first telescopes were made in the early 17th century. Soon, astronomers were using the new instrument to discover new planets and stars in the Universe.

NEBULA BY HUBBLE
This image was taken by Hubble *in 1995. It shows giant columns of gas and dust in the Eagle Nebula, 7,000* **light years** *from Earth.*

APERTURE
Light enters the telescope here. The door is closed when the telescope is not in use.

Aperture door

HARLAN J. SMITH TELESCOPE
Paving the way for the space-age Hubble, *this £3,000,000 telescope weighs more than 3 tonnes. Its primary mirror measures 2.7 metres in diameter.*

Nobody is sure who made the first telescope. However, we do know that Hans Lippershey (see page 23) made telescopes that used lenses. The reflecting telescope, which uses mirrors, was invented by the English physicist Isaac Newton (1642–1727). Swirling air currents in the atmosphere alter the view through telescopes. In 1990, this problem was solved by the launch of the *Hubble* Space Telescope. *Hubble* gives us incredibly clear views of the Universe from space. Some telescopes on Earth receive clear images by using computers to remove any distortions.

HUBBLE SPACE
TELESCOPE
HUBBLE'S MIRRORS COULD
'SEE' AN OBJECT THE SIZE
OF A PERSON 4,000
KILOMETRES AWAY.

*Hans Lippershey (1570–1619) worked
as a spectacle maker in Holland. It is
likely that Lippershey put two lenses
in front of each other, and saw a
magnified image. He used this
effect to build the first telescope.*

MAIN MIRROR

The primary mirror is 2.4
metres across. It collects
light and reflects it on to
the secondary mirror.
This reflects the light on
to the instruments.

Antenna

Secondary mirror

SOLAR CELLS

Two 12-metre solar panels
convert sunlight into the
electricity *Hubble* needs to
work. Spare electricity is
stored in batteries for use
when *Hubble* is in shade.

MAIN COMPUTERS

One computer controls
the instruments and
transmits a signal to the
ground. The other
operates the pointing
control system.

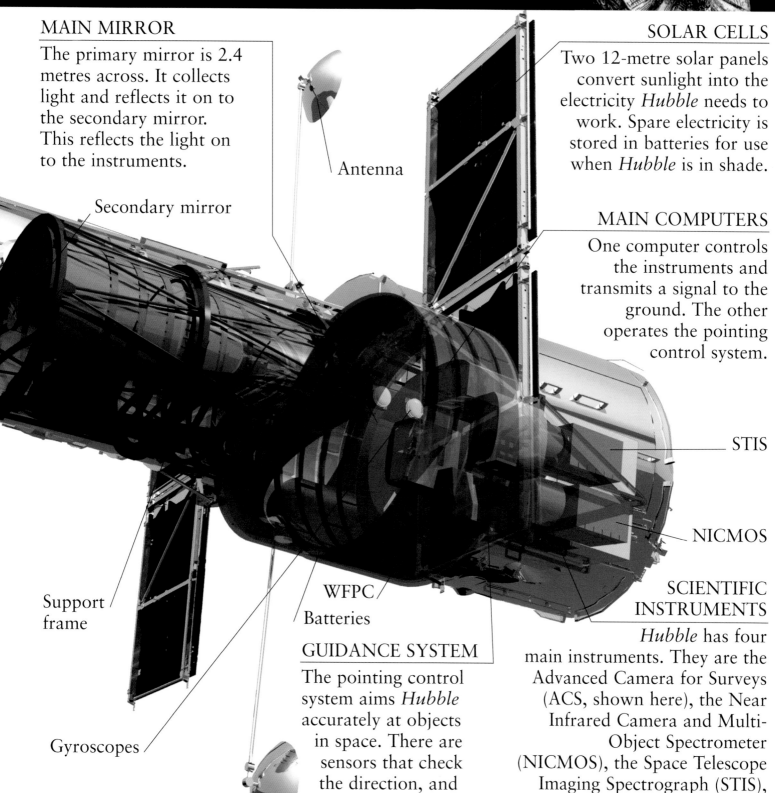

STIS

NICMOS

Support
frame

Gyroscopes

WFPC

Batteries

GUIDANCE SYSTEM

The pointing control
system aims *Hubble*
accurately at objects
in space. There are
sensors that check
the direction, and
actuators, which tilt
the telescope.

SCIENTIFIC
INSTRUMENTS

Hubble has four
main instruments. They are the
Advanced Camera for Surveys
(ACS, shown here), the Near
Infrared Camera and Multi-
Object Spectrometer
(NICMOS), the Space Telescope
Imaging Spectrograph (STIS),
and the Wide Field and
Planetary Camera (WFPC).

ELECTRIC MOTOR

THERE ARE PROBABLY 30 or more electric motors in your home. They work devices from toothbrushes and clocks, to vacuum cleaners and drills.

CHUCK

The drill bit is held firmly by the chuck. Tightening the chuck presses metal jaws on to the bit. This chuck is tightened by a key.

Drive shaft

Drill bit

BARLOW'S SPUR MOTOR
British physicist Peter Barlow (1776–1862) demonstrated this motor in 1822. Electricity flowing in the wheel between the magnets made the wheel turn.

An electric motor works using electromagnets. Danish physicist Hans Christian Oersted (1777–1851) discovered **electromagnetism** in 1820. He saw that a compass needle moved when the electricity in a nearby wire was switched on. The next year, Michael Faraday (see page 25) invented an electric motor. A simple electric motor has two main parts. In the centre are coils of wire on a rotor. Around it are fixed magnets. An electric current in the coils turns them into magnets. They attract and repel the fixed magnets, making the rotor spin.

Grip

ELECTRIC CAR
The experimental Eliica car is powered by electric motors. Electricity for the motors comes from rechargeable batteries. Eliica weighs 2.5 tonnes, but is faster than most sports cars. Its top speed is an incredible 370 km/h.

THE FIRST ELECTRIC HAND DRILL WAS BUILT IN 1895 BY A GERMAN INVENTOR NAMED WILHELN FEIN.

British physicist. He made important discoveries about electricity and magnetism. He built the first working electric motor and invented the electricity generator.

Speed setting switch

ELECTRIC MOTOR

The motor in a drill is called a universal motor. Electricity travels to the coils of wire in the rotor through a pair of contacts called a **commutator**.

Commutator

Brushes

Magnets

Copper coils

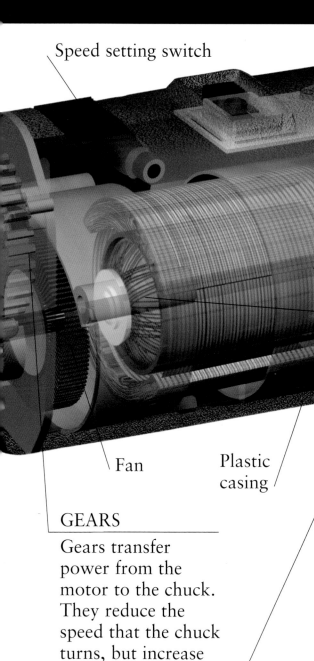

Fan

Plastic casing

GEARS

Gears transfer power from the motor to the chuck. They reduce the speed that the chuck turns, but increase the turning power.

SWITCH

The switch turns the motor on and off. It also controls the flow of the electricity, making the motor turn slow or fast.

Insulation

Power cable

Chuck key

GENERATORS

An electricity generator does the reverse job of a motor, turning movement into electricity. These generators are inside a hydroelectric power station where water movement is converted into electricity.

CAMERA

THE INVENTION OF THE CINE-CAMERA BEGAN THE movie industry. Cine-cameras record moving images on to strips of film. They were the only way to record movies until video recording was invented in the 1950s.

EARLY PHOTOGRAPHY
People in early photographs had to keep very still for up to eight minutes. This is why they were often pictured sitting down. Movement made the image blur.

In 1827, French inventor Joseph Niepce (1765–1833) took the first-ever photograph. It was recorded on a metal plate coated with light-sensitive chemicals. Moving photographs became possible in the 1880s, when film became good enough to record a photograph in a split second. Then, American inventor Thomas Edison (1847–1931) built the first cine-camera. The Lumières (see page 27) used a similar machine to record movies. Electronic television cameras were developed in the 1920s, but their pictures could not be recorded until the 1950s. Video cameras were developed in the 1970s, and digital video cameras in the 1980s.

HIGH-DEFINITION VIDEO
State-of-the-art video cameras record digital high-definition video. Film makers are using them instead of film cameras.

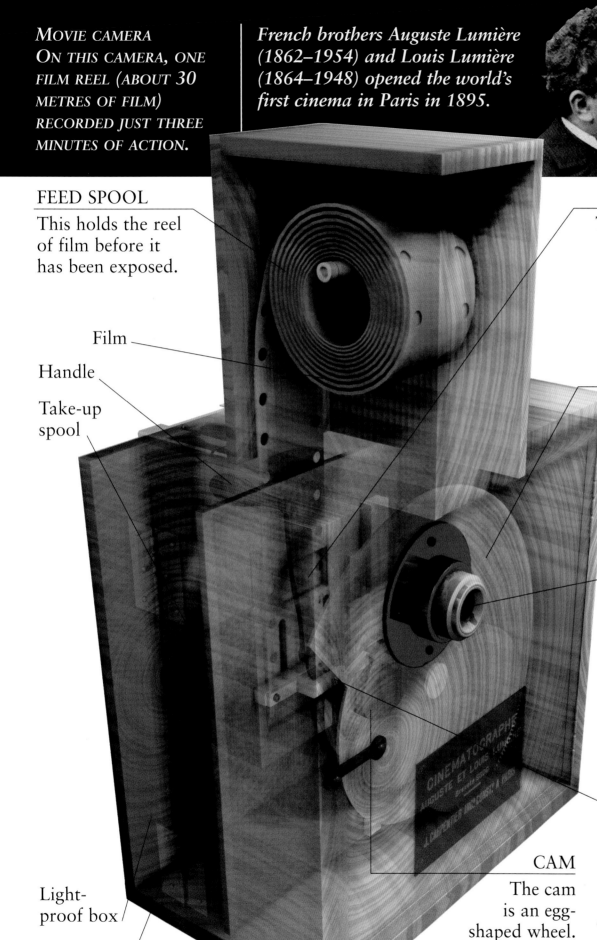

French brothers Auguste Lumière (1862–1954) and Louis Lumière (1864–1948) opened the world's first cinema in Paris in 1895.

FEED SPOOL

This holds the reel of film before it has been exposed.

Film

Handle

Take-up spool

Light-proof box

Camera rear door

GATE

The film moves down through the gate. It stops briefly for a frame to be recorded on it, then moves to the next frame.

SHUTTER

The shutter opens when the film is stopped in the gate. This lets light hit the film and record a frame.

LENS

The lens gathers light from the scene. It bends the light and focuses it on to the film in the gate.

CLAW

The claw is a mechanism that pulls the film down through the gate one frame at a time. Throughout the silent movie era, the claw pulled through 16 frames per second.

CAM

The cam is an egg-shaped wheel. As it turns round the 'bump' pushes the claw up and down.

COMPUTER

THE COMPUTER IS PROBABLY THE MOST USEFUL machine ever invented. It can perform almost any job we program it to do. For example, we use computers for sending e-mails, writing, and looking at photographs. Computers also fly aircraft, help diagnose illnesses, and work games consoles.

In the 19th century, Charles Babbage (see below) designed a mechanical computer. The first electric computers were built in the 1940s. They took up whole rooms, but were less powerful than modern-day calculators. After the transistor was invented in 1948, computers became faster, cheaper, and more reliable. The integrated circuit (microchip) was invented in 1958. This allowed complex circuits to be squeezed into a tiny space. The first microprocessor chip was launched in 1972, and the first personal computers were developed soon afterwards. The first version of Microsoft Windows™ appeared in 1985.

BABBAGE'S MACHINE
This is a modern model of a calculating machine designed in the 1820s by Charles Babbage (1792–1871). It was too complicated to build at the time.

KEYBOARD
The keyboard is for typing text and numbers into the computer. It is also used for controlling the computer.

MONITOR
The monitor displays text, images, video, and other information held on the computer.

MOUSE
The mouse controls the position of a pointer on the screen. The pointer is used to choose things on the screen. The mouse uses either motion-sensitive wheels, or a light, to detect movement.

OPTICAL DRIVE

The optical drive reads and writes information on CD-ROM and DVD discs.

CENTRAL PROCESSING UNIT

The CPU is the computer's 'brain'. It sorts out information and controls all the other computer parts.

POWER SUPPLY

The power supply provides electricity for the circuits, hard drive motors, and cooling fans.

MOTHERBOARD

All the computer's electronic circuits are attached to the motherboard. The main microchip on the board is called the processor. This is like the computer's brain.

Fan

HARD DRIVE

The hard drive stores programmes and information. They are saved even when the computer is turned off.

Video card

Sound card

Modem card

MEMORY BOARD

Programmes and information are loaded in the computer's memory when it is turned on. The memory is called random access memory (RAM).

Speaker

GLOSSARY

actuator
A device that makes part of a machine move.

aviator
A person who flies aircraft.

avionics
Electronic circuits that help a pilot to fly and navigate an aircraft.

cellular
A telephone network used for mobile telephones.

combustion
Another word for burning.

commutator
A device that changes the flow of electricity.

computer language
A list of instructions written in a language that a computer can understand.

diesel engine
An internal combustion engine that uses an oil called diesel oil as its fuel.

electromagnetism
When an electric current creates a magnet, or a moving magnet creates an electric current.

ethyl alcohol
A liquid often used as a fuel, made from sugar.

exhaust
Gases that come out of an engine.

gas engine
An internal combustion engine that uses a gas as its fuel.

gears
Sets of toothed wheels that allow an engine to turn a vehicle's wheels at different speeds.

glider
An aircraft without an engine, which gains height by flying in rising air currents, or by being towed by another aircraft.

gyroscope
A navigation device with a heavy spinning flywheel inside. The wheel always stays at the same angle.

internal combustion engine
An engine in which the fuel burns in spaces inside the engine, such as the diesel engine and petrol engine.

kilobyte
A measure of computer memory.

light year
The distance that light travels in a year, which is about 9.5 million million kilometres.

liquid oxygen
Oxgyen that is cooled and pressurised to turn it into liquid.

locomotive
A machine that pulls or pushes railway carriages or trucks.

mass production
Making objects in large quantities, normally on a production line, where pieces are added to the objects as they move through a factory.

navigate
To find the way from place to place.

nebula
A giant cloud of gas and dust in space.

network
Pathways that connect things together, such as the links between telephones.

petrol engine
An internal combustion engine that uses a liquid called petrol as its fuel.

pneumatic
Using air or another gas to work, such as an air-filled tyre.

radar
A device that detects objects in the air by sending out radio waves and detecting any waves that bounce back.

self-propelled
A vehicle with an engine, that moves along under its own power.

stabilator
A combined elevator (which controls the up-and-down movement of the nose) and horizontal stabiliser (which helps the aircraft to balance).

static electricity
Electricity that clings to an object's surface, rather than flowing through it.

thrust
The push made by a jet engine.

turbofan
A type of jet engine used by most modern jet aircraft.

vacuum
A space almost without any sort of gas.

INDEX